WILLIAMSON W PUBLISHING

KIDS' EASY
Knitting Projects

Peg Blanchette

Illustrations by MARC NADEL

Quick Starts for Kids!™

WILLIAMSON PUBLISHING ★ CHARLOTTE, VERMONT

LIBRARY OF CONGRESS CATALOGING-IN-PUBLICATION DATA

Blanchette, Peg, 1949-
    Kids' easy knitting projects / Peg Blanchette: illustrations by Marc Nadel
        p. cm. — (Williamson quick starts for kids! book)
    ISBN 1-885593-48-1 (pbk.)
        1. Knitting—Juvenile literature. 2. Knitting—Patterns—Juvenile
literature. [1. Knitting. 2. Knitting--Patterns.] I. Nadel, Marc. II. Title.
    III. Series.
TT820 .B645 2000
746.43'2—dc21   00-043496

Quick Starts for Kids!® series editor: **Susan Williamson**
Interior design: **Bonnie Atwater**
Interior illustrations: **Marc Nadel**
Cover design: **Marie Ferrante-Doyle**
Cover illustrations: **Michael Kline**
Cover photography: **David A. Seaver**
Printing: **Capital City Press**

Williamson Publishing Co.
P.O. Box 185
Charlotte, VT 05445
(800) 234-8791

Manufactured in the United States of America

10 9 8

DEDICATION

To my grandmother, Helen, who passed her love of knitting to me; to my husband, Joe, for loving me and supporting my crafting projects (no matter how bizarre); and to my best friend, Terri, for sharing so many adventures and making them so much fun.

Contents

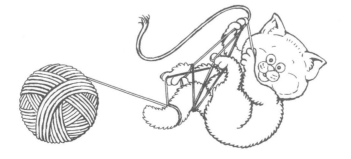

Quick Starts Knitting!

Creating something by yourself is the greatest! Knitting just seems to get those creative juices flowing. You'll find that once you get the basics down, you'll put your own personal style into everything you make.

★ **Let the look and feel of different yarns inspire you.**

Do you like lightweight, delicate yarns or bold, bulky yarns? Dangling beads or colorful tassels? No need for your project to look *exactly* like the ones here. In each of these crafts, there's lots of room to add your own creative touches.

★ **Where should you begin?**

If you're a first-time knitter, I suggest you begin with the coasters (page 19) and scarf (pages 20–29), which teach the basics. Then, pick and choose. Once you've chosen a project, gather your materials. And be sure to include the most important one — your imagination!

Quick Starts
MATERIALS

THE BASICS

Crochet Hook

Crochet hooks are great for picking up dropped stitches, picking up stitches along the bound-off edges of a knitted piece, and adding tassels or pom-poms.

Knitting Needles

Knitting needles are available, straight or round, in all different sizes, lengths, and materials. Here's a hint to help you choose the ones that are right for you: The thinner your needles (with the lower number), the smaller your stitches will be. So, if you'd like to knit a very fine piece with small, delicate stitches, choose the thinner needles. If you're after a bolder look, the big, thick needles are what you want.

Safety Pins

If your pattern calls for knitting nine stitches, purling two, and then repeating those two steps, you can use safety pins as stitch markers so you know when you have to switch back and forth.

Scissors

Look for blunt-edged scissors; they're sharp enough to cut through yarn and safe, too.

Tape Measure

This is almost a necessity because you'll need to take measurements while working on your project. A ruler can work just as well in most cases.

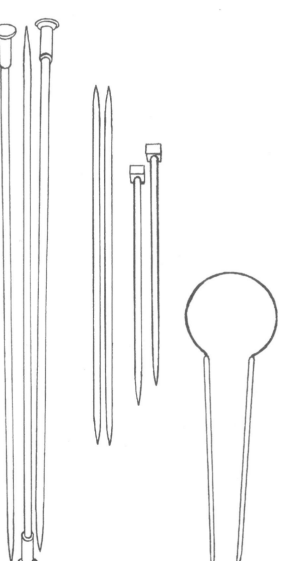

Yarn

Yarns come in many kinds, colors, textures, and thicknesses, but the one thing they all have in common is that they are grouped according to *weight:*

Baby yarn is extremely lightweight.

Sport yarn is lightweight.

Worsted yarn is medium weight.

Bulky yarn is heavyweight.

The *ply* refers to the number of strands twisted together to form the thickness (2-ply, 3-ply, or 4-ply), but the weight is more important when picking out a suitable yarn for your project.

Yarn usually comes in pull-out *skeins* (SKAYNS). The end you begin with should be peeking out from the inside of the skein. (If the end is hidden inside, you may have to search for it.)

If you're buying more than one skein of the same color, always read the label to make sure you buy the same *dye lot* numbers. Otherwise, there may be slight color variations noticeable in your finished piece.

The label provides you with the ply, the weight, and any special instructions you may need, such as how to wash it.

Quick Starts Tips!™

EASY ON THE EYES

Using a light-colored yarn will enable you to see each stitch more easily.

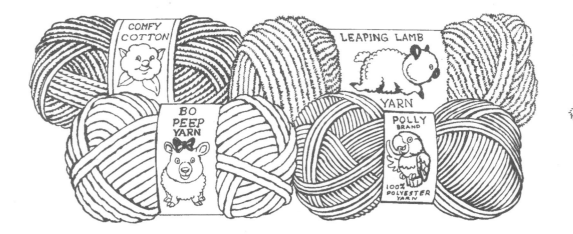

Yarn Needle

Also called an embroidery needle, this needle is used to weave in yarn ends, work embroidery stitches, thread beads, join seams, and add those finishing touches that will make your piece extra special!

Quick Starts Tips!™

ROLLING A SKEIN INTO A BALL

If you wind your yarn into a ball, the yarn is less likely to become tangled while you work on your project. Starting with a small piece of crumpled paper, gradually pull the yarn from the skein as you wrap it around the paper. Continue winding until you have a large ball of yarn.

It's As Simple As . . .

If you can do these four things — and you will be able to in no time flat — you can knit. Really! So here we go!

Let's clarify:

★ In the drawings, the knitted yarn is light colored, and the working yarn is shaded.

★ In the text, any word in all capital letters is defined and illustrated in our *Quick Starts Illustrated Stitch & How-to Dictionary* on pages 59–62, unless otherwise indicated.

Casting On

Casting on is the name for putting stitches on the needle.

Step 1:

Pull a strand of yarn — figure about 1" (2.5 cm) per stitch. For example, if the pattern calls for 40 stitches, pull 40" (100 cm), plus an extra 5" (12.5 cm) for a tail.

Step 2:

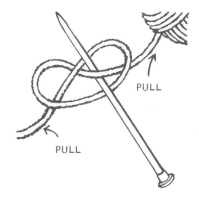

Make a loop in the yarn just after the measured length. Pick up a knitting needle with your right hand (see note, page 10) and push the needle through the loop as shown. Pull it firmly, but not tightly. There's your first stitch!

PULL

PULL

Step 3:

Holding the yarn you've measured in your left hand, wrap a strand around your left thumb as shown. With the thumb acting as the left needle, insert the right needle as shown.

THUMB ACTS AS
LEFT NEEDLE

MEASURED YARN

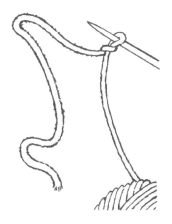

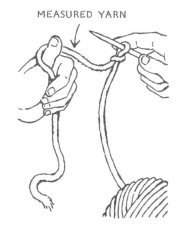

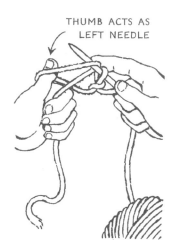

Step 4:

From the back, bring the yarn from the ball or skein, called the WORKING YARN, to the front between your left thumb and the right needle. Wrap it to the right as shown. Now, loop the yarn from your left thumb over the tip of the right needle. Pull the yarn in your left hand so that a stitch forms on the knitting needle.

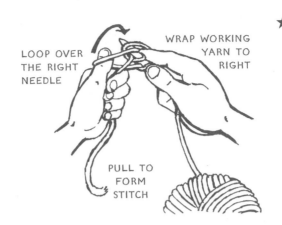

LOOP OVER THE RIGHT NEEDLE

WRAP WORKING YARN TO RIGHT

PULL TO FORM STITCH

★ **NOTE:** It doesn't matter whether you are right- or left-handed. You use both hands in knitting, so follow the directions as written.

Does it feel a little awkward? That's probably because you've never done this before. With a little time, you won't believe how easy it becomes! So repeat steps 3 and 4 until you have as many stitches on the right-hand needle as you want. (You can slip them off the needle and simply pull them out to keep practicing for a while.)

Bravo! You've just cast on a row of knitted stitches! Now it's time to work with both needles.

. . . **QUICK STARTS JUMP-STARTS™**

Help! I'm stuck already!

If you feel like you're all thumbs, stop, take a breath, and think about the steps.

★ Try them one more time.

★ Illustrations aren't helpful? Maybe you aren't a visual person, so try just following the words. Once you get it, go over it again while looking at the illustrations so you can "see" how to do it too!

★ Still stuck? Ask for some help. Lots of people knit (and they all were confused at first). Ask a teacher, a librarian, someone who works in a craft store, or a neighbor. (People love to share what they know.)

Hang in there. I know you'll be off to a fine start soon!

The Knit Stitch

Step 1:

Hold the needle with the cast-on stitches in your left hand. Insert the tip of the right-hand needle through the first stitch, *under* the left-hand needle.

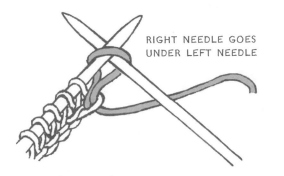

RIGHT NEEDLE GOES UNDER LEFT NEEDLE

Step 2:

Hold the WORKING YARN (shaded) between your right index finger and thumb. From underneath, bring it over the tip of the right-hand needle and slip it in between the right and left needles.

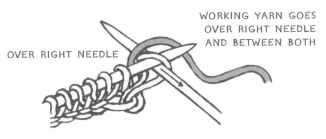

OVER RIGHT NEEDLE

WORKING YARN GOES OVER RIGHT NEEDLE AND BETWEEN BOTH

Step 3:

Pull the right needle toward you slightly, hooking the WORKING YARN with the tip of the right needle as shown. Bring the yarn through the stitch from underneath, while the right needle crosses *over* the left one. You've slipped the new stitch onto the right needle.

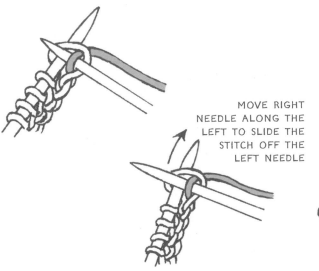

MOVE RIGHT NEEDLE ALONG THE LEFT TO SLIDE THE STITCH OFF THE LEFT NEEDLE

Step 4:

Continue down the row, carefully following steps 1 through 3, as shown.

NEW STITCH IS NOW ON THE RIGHT NEEDLE

When all the stitches are on the right needle, one row has been worked. How does it look — a little uneven, or nice and smooth?

SLOW, STEADY!

To knit an even edge, try not to pull or tug at the stitches (that makes the edge of your piece look ragged). Always work the first row (the row after your cast-on row) slowly, carefully pulling each new stitch off the left needle.

*N*ow that you've worked one row, you're ready to switch your needles so that the one with the stitches is in your left hand and the right needle is free to start another row. Keep knitting stitches and rows until you feel comfortable with the feel of the needle movement. Like anything else you practice, it'll become easier the more you do it!

The Purl Stitch

Once you've mastered the KNIT STITCH, the PURL STITCH will seem quite easy. The secret to the purl stitch is to make certain that you insert your right needle correctly. (After that, you'll probably recognize the steps.)

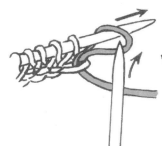

KNIT

WHEN YOU KNIT, THE TIP OF YOUR RIGHT NEEDLE ENTERS EACH STITCH FACING IN THE *SAME* DIRECTION AS THE TIP OF THE LEFT NEEDLE.

PURL

WHEN YOU PURL, BE CAREFUL TO INSERT THE TIP OF YOUR RIGHT NEEDLE INTO EACH STITCH FROM THE *OPPOSITE* DIRECTION!

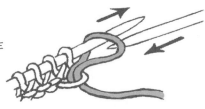

Step 1:

Hold the WORKING YARN *in front of* the piece and insert the right needle through the first stitch from the back. (If you rest the left needle against your left index finger, you can use your left thumb to hold the right needle in place.)

Step 2:

Using your right hand, bring the WORKING YARN around the right needle.

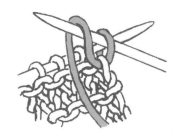

Step 3:

Back the right needle out, hooking the WORKING YARN through the stitch with the tip of the right needle. Slide the new stitch onto the right needle.

Repeat the three purling steps until all the stitches have been worked across the row.

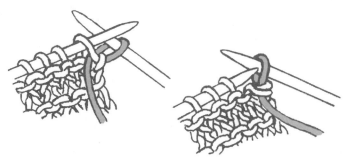

Here's where you may notice another difference between knitting and purling. When knitting, you start with the right needle behind the left needle and end up with the right needle in front of the left one. But when purling, the right needle starts in front of the left needle and ends up behind the left needle.

Quick Starts Tips!™

LOOSEN UP!

Sometimes when you're working a row, you may find it difficult to slide your needles inside the stitches because you've stitched them so tightly. If you give the WORKING YARN a little tug as you're sliding the stitch from the left needle to the right, you'll create a looser stitch that's easier to work.

KNIT BIND OFF

Step 1:

Knit two stitches. Insert the left needle into the front of the first knitted stitch on the right needle and pull it over the second stitch. Now you should have only one stitch on the right needle.

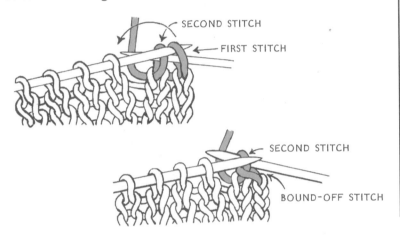

SECOND STITCH

FIRST STITCH

SECOND STITCH

BOUND-OFF STITCH

Step 2:

Knit another stitch onto the right needle (don't forget to make the stitches loose enough so you can work them easily). Insert the left needle into the front of the first stitch on the right needle and pull it over the stitch you just knitted. Continue this process until there's only one stitch left on your needle.

LOCKING THE BIND OFF

Pull the remaining stitch on the needle to make a very loose loop. Cut the WORKING YARN, bring it through the loop, and pull it tightly. Then, WEAVE IN the remaining piece of working yarn into the seams.

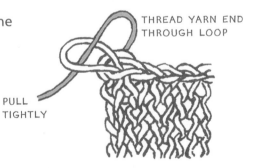

THREAD YARN END THROUGH LOOP

PULL TIGHTLY

PURL BIND OFF

Step 1:

Purl two stitches. Insert the left needle into the front of the first purled stitch and pull it over the second stitch.

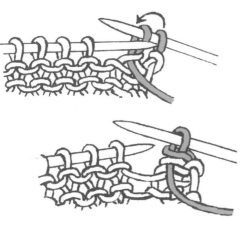

Step 2:

Purl another stitch; insert the left needle into the front of the first stitch on the right needle and pull it over the stitch just purled. Continue this process until there's only one stitch left on your needle.

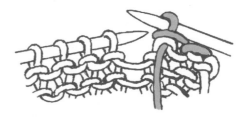

Now, you can lock the bind off in the same way you did for the knitted stitches. Pull the remaining stitch on the needle to make a very loose loop. Cut the WORKING YARN, bring it through the loop, and pull it tightly. Finally, WEAVE IN the remaining piece of working yarn into the seams.

Great job! You've learned a lot so far. If you feel comfortable moving ahead to learn more, keep going! If you feel you need a little more practice, knit and purl away!

BINDING OFF A COMBINATION OF STITCHES

The bind-off instructions seem easy enough when you're knitting across one whole row or purling across a row. Use the knit bind off or the purl bind off. What do you do if a pattern calls for knit and purl stitches in the same row? Do you knit or purl to bind off?

In cases like this, you FOLLOW THE PATTERN. Let's say your last row calls for alternately knitting two stitches and then purling two stitches across the row.

1. To bind off, knit two stitches onto the right needle and bind off the first stitch as you normally would.

2. Now, position the WORKING YARN to purl (bring it in front of the piece). Purl one stitch. Next, bind off the first stitch on your right needle. Purl the second stitch. Then bind off the first stitch on your right needle again.

3. Now, reposition your yarn so that you can knit again (bring it to the back of your piece). Knit one stitch; then bind off one stitch. Knit your second stitch and bind off one stitch.

4. Reposition the yarn again to start purling. Purl one; bind off the first on the right needle. Purl your second and bind off one.

Beginning to detect a pattern? Continue alternating knitting and purling until your row is bound off.

READING KNITTING PATTERNS

The pattern instructions for stitch combinations usually appear between asterisks (*) in a kind of "shorthand." Take a look at the following instructions:

Row 1:
Knit 2, *Knit 2, Purl 1, Knit 2 together*; repeat * 3 times, Knit 2

Row 2:
Purl across

This is what those directions mean:

Row 1:
First, knit two stitches.

Next, knit two stitches, purl one stitch, and then knit two stitches together. Repeat this three-part combination three times.

Finally, knit two more stitches.

Row 2:
Purl across the row.

And We're Off ...

QUICK STARTS
COASTERS!

Using size 7 needles, CAST ON 20 stitches of any scrap yarn.

KNIT all stitches across 38 rows.

BIND OFF all stitches.

Guess what? You've just made a coaster! Make a bunch of them in different colors and give them as gifts or SEW THE SEAMS together to make a cozy lap quilt. Want to make it thicker? Use bulky weight yarn.

Now, practice the PURL STITCH in the same way.

Wool Scarf
with Beaded Fringe

Style your scarf by the stitch pattern of your choice, by using multicolored yarn, tweedy yarn, or a soft, solid-colored yarn, and by the type of fringe that you choose to add.

Here we make a scarf with beaded fringe, but you can add any type of fringe you like. If beads are your style, I suggest using *pony beads* because their larger size makes them easier to work with.

Materials:

1 pair straight knitting needles, size 10

5-oz (125 g) skein of bulky yarn, 2

Measuring tape or ruler

Crochet hook

Yarn needle

Package of craft beads (pony size); optional

It's as simple as . . .

CAST ON (page 9)

KNIT STITCH (page 12)

PURL STITCH (page 14)

BIND OFF (page 16)

★ NOTE: When you see a word in capital letters, it means that the definition and a how-to illustration can be found in our *Quick Starts Illustrated Stitch & How-to Dictionary* on pages 59–62, unless otherwise indicated.

Scarf Sizing:

This is a rough estimate of typical scarf lengths:

For kids ages 3 to 6:
anywhere from 24" (61 cm) to 36" (92 cm) long

For kids ages 7 to 12:
anywhere from 30" (75 cm) to 40" (100 cm) long

For teenagers and adults:
anywhere from 40" (100 cm) to 63" (157.5 cm) long

For an 18-inch (45 cm) doll or teddy bear:
anywhere from 14" (36 cm) to 18" (45 cm) long

Here's the *basic pattern* for the Wool Scarf with Beaded Fringe:

Row 1:
Knit 2, Purl 2; repeat * to end of row, ending with Purl 2

Row 2:
Repeat row 1

Row 3:
Purl 2, Knit 2; repeat * to end of row, ending with Knit 2

Row 4:
Repeat row 3

★ NOTE: *Remember when READING PATTERNS that the pattern falls between the two asterisks (*). So, *Knit 2, Purl 2* is a single pattern step, even though it is made up of two stitches. See page 18 for more help with patterns.*

1. CAST ON 24 stitches. Then, work in the pattern (repeating rows 1–4) until the scarf measures 40" (100 cm). If you want a longer scarf, just keep on knitting in the pattern until you feel like stopping!

2. When the scarf is finished, BIND OFF all stitches. As you bind off, KNIT and PURL the row as if you were still working in the pattern stitch (see "Binding Off a Combination of Stitches," pages 17–18). WEAVE IN the loose ends.

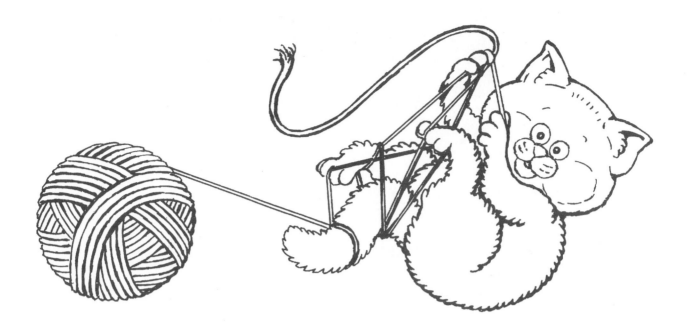

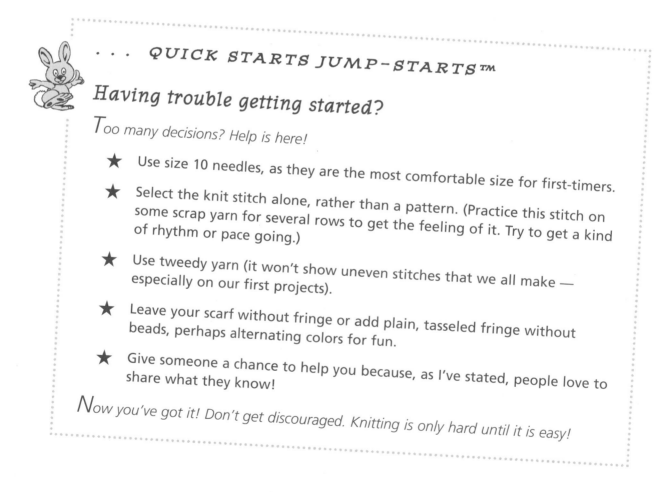

· · · QUICK STARTS JUMP–STARTS™

Having trouble getting started?

Too many decisions? Help is here!

★ Use size 10 needles, as they are the most comfortable size for first-timers.

★ Select the knit stitch alone, rather than a pattern. (Practice this stitch on some scrap yarn for several rows to get the feeling of it. Try to get a kind of rhythm or pace going.)

★ Use tweedy yarn (it won't show uneven stitches that we all make — especially on our first projects).

★ Leave your scarf without fringe or add plain, tasseled fringe without beads, perhaps alternating colors for fun.

★ Give someone a chance to help you because, as I've stated, people love to share what they know!

Now you've got it! Don't get discouraged. Knitting is only hard until it is easy!

DROPPED STITCHES!

*H*ave no fear; the dropped-stitch repair method is here! Yes, we're all stitch droppers, so one of the first things every knitter learns is how to pick up what you dropped. (Sound familiar?) Here's what you do:

If the error occurs in the row you're working, or one row below the current one, you can "unknit" until you've reached the stitch that was dropped.

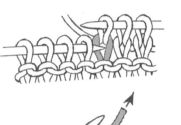

To unknit knit stitches, hold the knitted piece in your right hand and insert the left needle into the loop *just below* the first stitch to be unknit. Move this loop from the right onto the left needle. Then, gently pull out the stitch. You've just unknit a stitch! Continue unknitting until you've reached the dropped stitch.

(If you want to unknit purl stitches, insert the left needle the same way you did when you unknit the knit stitches, picking up the loop just below the stitch to be unknit. This time, be sure to insert the left needle *in front of* the right one.)

Now, place the dropped stitch back on the left needle and continue knitting. There you have it — and when all is said and done, no one is the wiser for it!

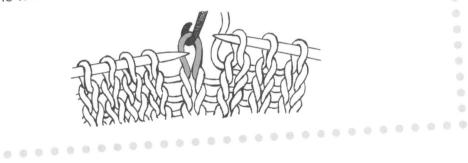

*Quick Starts Tips!*™

POSITIONING THE YARN

Each time you switch between knitting and purling, you'll need to move your yarn. Remember that when you knit, the WORKING YARN is always in back of the piece, while to purl, the working yarn is always in front of the piece. So, after you knit the second stitch of the pattern, bring the yarn in front of the piece, as shown. Then, after you purl the second stitch of the pattern, move the yarn again so it's in back of the piece. You'll be ready to knit two more stitches and keep on going until the pattern is complete!

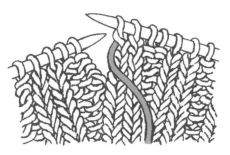

BRING THE YARN IN *FRONT* AFTER YOU HAVE KNITTED THE SECOND PATTERN STITCH

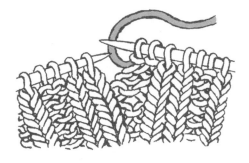

MOVE THE YARN TO THE *BACK* AFTER YOU PURL THE SECOND PATTERN STITCH

Making tasseled fringe

1. Cut a piece of cardboard 3" x 12" (7.5 x 30 cm). Loosely wind the yarn around the cardboard 20 times for 20 strands of yarn — the same number as stitches you cast on. (They can be the same color as the scarf, a complimentary color, or two colors, such as using yarns that are the same two colors in your tweed.) Cut the yarn across one end.

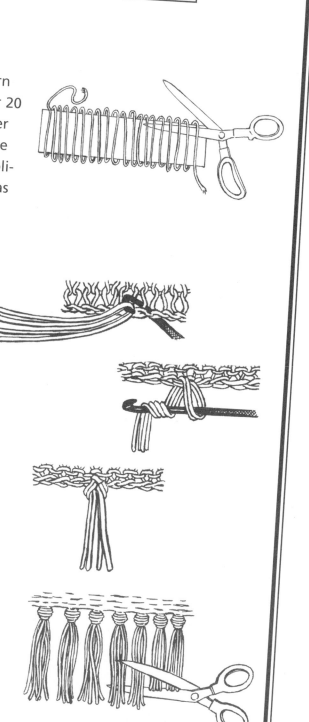

2. Take two strands of the cut yarn and fold them in half. Using a crochet hook, draw the folded end through one of the bottom stitches on one of the short ends of the scarf. Then, pull the loose ends through the folded end.

3. Pull the loose ends tightly to form a knot. Repeat this step until you have evenly spaced sets of fringe across the short ends of the scarf.

4. Turn the scarf over and lay the fringe on a table. Cut the loose ends so they are even. You now have wonderful fringe that can be left as is, beaded (page 28), or BRAIDED (page 59).

❋ FINISHING TOUCHES ❋

Adding the beads

1. Thread the yarn needle with two strands of a fringe set and slide a bead onto the strands.

   Repeat with as many beads as you want on the fringe (I used five). Set aside.

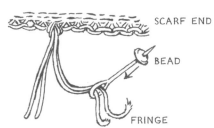

SCARF END

BEAD

FRINGE

2. Thread the next two strands of yarn (from the same set you just worked with) through the yarn needle and slide on the beads. Take the loose ends of the first two strands of beaded yarn and tie a knot with the loose ends of the strands you just beaded.

3. Pull tightly to form a very sturdy knot. Continue down the line of fringe on both ends of the scarf until all strands have been beaded. Wow! Your scarf looks great!

Fringe Fun!

Here are three popular fringes that you can make:

BEADED   BRAIDED   TASSELED

s t r e t c h
your creative muscles!

- *Add a simple design* to the middle of your scarf.

- *Embroider someone's initials* into a scarf you make for her.

- *Make a shawl* with circular needles by knitting a wider and longer piece (24" x 64"/ 60 x 160 cm) out of a soft yarn!

Cozy-Toe Slippers

One of the first things my grand-mother taught me to knit was a pair of slippers. Over the years I've made lots and lots of them. My friends keep me busy with requests for more. I now make them with colors to match winter holidays from Thanksgiving straight through Valentine's Day. You name it, and I'll find a color to suit the season ... and the reason! There's a basket by my door filled with slippers for friends to use to keep their tootsies warm while visiting me during our cold Vermont winters.

Materials:

This project is done with two strands of yarn (DOUBLED-UP YARN) to make the slippers thick and comfy. (See *Quick Starts Tips!*™, page 32.)

1 pair straight knitting needles, size 9 (for adult slippers) or size 8 (for child slippers)

3-oz (75 g) skein of 4-ply wool blend yarn, 2

Yarn needle

Crochet hook

Decorations for slipper top (optional)

It's as simple as . . .

CAST ON (page 9)

KNIT STITCH (page 12)

PURL STITCH (page 14)

OVERCAST STITCH (page 62)

Here are the *basic patterns* for
Cozy-Toe Slippers:

PATTERN #1
Row 1:
Knit 9, Purl 1, Knit 9, Purl 1, Knit 9

Row 2:
Knit all stitches

PATTERN #2
Row 1:
Knit 1, Purl 1; repeat * to end of row

Row 2:
Purl 1, Knit 1; repeat * to end of row

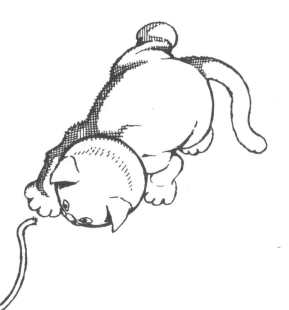

Quick Starts Tips!™

DOUBLING UP YARN

I've doubled up the yarn strands for some of the projects. Doubling up the yarn creates thick and sturdy finished pieces, which is great for purses, slippers, and scarves that will get a lot of wear. And by doubling up yarn, you can combine your favorite colors. To do this, simply take two strands of yarn from two different skeins and work with them as if they were one strand, holding them together as you work your piece.

1. CAST ON 29 stitches with DOUBLED-UP YARN and work in pattern #1, repeating rows 1 and 2 until you have 20 ridges.

2. Then, work in pattern #2 for 3" (7.5 cm).

3. Cut the yarn, leaving a long tail (to sew up the slipper top seam). Thread a yarn needle with the tail and work it back through the stitches remaining on the knitting needle.

Once the stitches have been transferred to the yarn needle, remove the knitting needle and pull the tail tightly to close up the toe end. Turn the slipper inside out. Use the OVERCAST STITCH to SEW THE SEAM of the slipper top until you reach the ridges.

4. Thread the yarn needle with the yarn tail at the slipper heel. Sew up the back seam with the OVERCAST STITCH and WEAVE IN the yarn tail. Turn your slipper right side out and it's ready to wear! Unless, that is, you'd like to add some finishing touches.

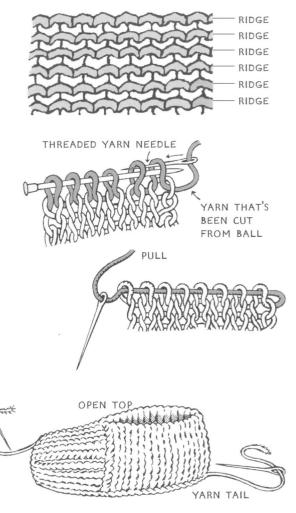

LOOSE ENDS

REMEMBER: *Always WEAVE IN yarn ends on the inside of your project so they don't show on the outside when you wear it.*

Quick and easy pom-poms

8" (20 CM)
PIECE OF YARN

1. Cut a piece of cardboard 2" x 5" (5 x 12.5 cm). Make one slit at each end. Cut a piece of yarn 8" (20 cm) and lay it across the cardboard, slipping each end through a slit to secure it.

2. Starting with a large ball of scrap yarn, wrap strands around the cardboard about 50 times. Cut off excess. Then, take the ends of yarn from the slits and knot them tightly around the wrapped yarn at the top of the cardboard. Cut the yarn across the bottom. Remove the cardboard, grab the ends of the knotted piece and shake it to fluff up the pom-pom. Place the pom-pom on top of the slipper. Push the crochet hook from inside the slipper out to the top, grab the yarn ends, and pull them through. Knot them on the inside to secure the pom-pom.

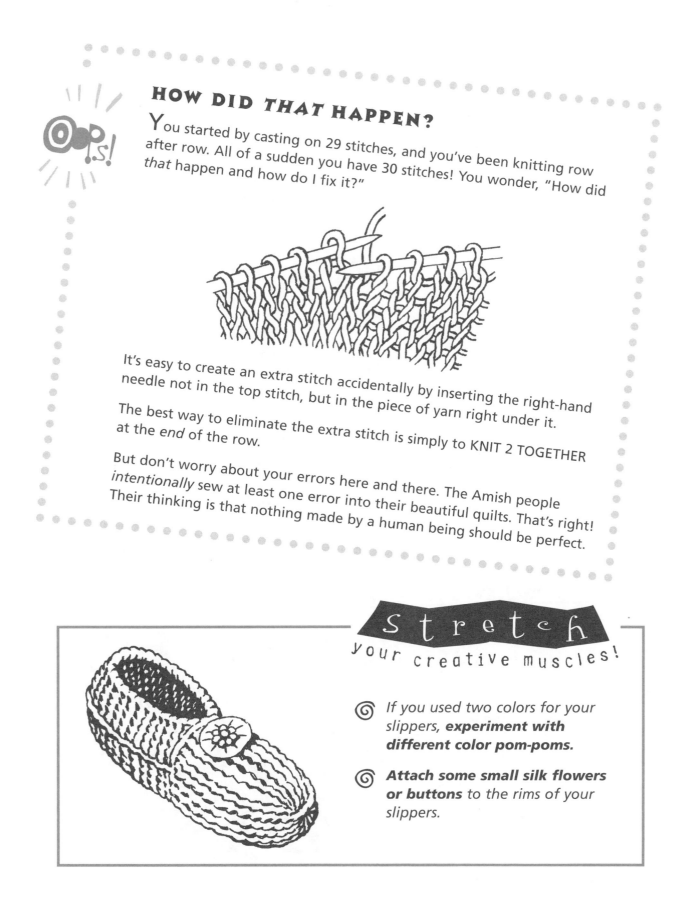

HOW DID THAT HAPPEN?

You started by casting on 29 stitches, and you've been knitting row after row. All of a sudden you have 30 stitches! You wonder, "How did that happen and how do I fix it?"

It's easy to create an extra stitch accidentally by inserting the right-hand needle not in the top stitch, but in the piece of yarn right under it.

The best way to eliminate the extra stitch is simply to KNIT 2 TOGETHER at the *end* of the row.

But don't worry about your errors here and there. The Amish people *intentionally* sew at least one error into their beautiful quilts. That's right! Their thinking is that nothing made by a human being should be perfect.

Stretch
your creative muscles!

- If you used two colors for your slippers, **experiment with different color pom-poms.**

- **Attach some small silk flowers or buttons** to the rims of your slippers.

Mama and Little Baa

Do you love soft, cuddly stuffed animals? Well then, here's a treat for you! What could be cuter than making your own Mama lamb with a little baby?

These make perfect gifts, too, for someone who is sick or feeling lonely or is just a special friend.

Accessorize your lamb by making a beaded necklace or attaching a tiny bell to its ear. Or, knit a tiny scarf for your lamb to wear!

It's as simple as . . .

CAST ON (page 9)

KNIT STITCH (page 12)

BIND OFF (page 16)

OVERCAST STITCH (page 62)

Materials:

1 pair straight knitting needles, size 10

3-oz (75 g) skein off-white wool yarn
(Mama lamb)

3-oz (75 g) skein black wool yarn
(Little Baa lamb)

Fleece stuffing

Yarn needle

Black felt for eyelashes

Glue

Off-white or black felt for ears

Ribbon for collar

Bell for collar (optional)

Here's the *basic pattern* for Mama and Little Baa:

Knit all rows

... QUICK STARTS JUMP-STARTS™

*T*he main instructions provided here are for the larger Mama. When you're ready to knit Little Baa, you can use the numbers in parentheses. For example, "CAST ON 72 (36) stitches" means to CAST ON 72 stitches when you're knitting Mama and 36 stitches when you're knitting Little Baa.

QUICK STARTS
how-to-knit-it

1. CAST ON 72 (36) stitches.

2. Knit 20 (10) rows.

3. BIND OFF 16 (8) stitches at the beginning of the next row; then, knit the rest of the stitches in that row. There should be 56 (28) stitches remaining on the needle.

4. At the beginning of the next row, BIND OFF another 16 (8) stitches and knit the remainder of the row. Now there should be 40 (20) stitches on the needle.

5. Knit 16 (8) rows.

6. CAST ON 16 (8) stitches at the beginning of the next row, using the method described at right to cast on stitches.

   There should be 56 (28) stitches remaining on the needle after you've knit the rest of the row.

7. At the beginning of the next row, CAST ON another 16 (8) stitches, using the same method. When you're done, there should be 72 (36) stitches on your needle.

8. Knit 20 (10) rows.

9. BIND OFF 24 (12) stitches at the beginning of the next row. After you knit the rest of the row, there should be 48 (24) stitches on the needle.

10. At the beginning of the next row, BIND OFF another 24 (12) stitches. There should be 24 (12) stitches remaining on the needle when you're finished.

11. Knit 24 (12) rows.

12. BIND OFF all stitches.

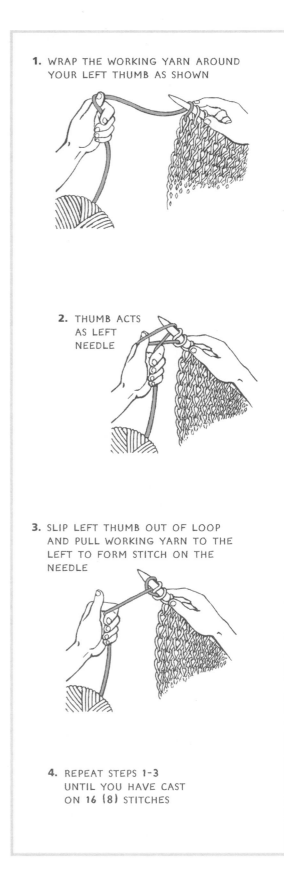

1. WRAP THE WORKING YARN AROUND YOUR LEFT THUMB AS SHOWN

2. THUMB ACTS AS LEFT NEEDLE

3. SLIP LEFT THUMB OUT OF LOOP AND PULL WORKING YARN TO THE LEFT TO FORM STITCH ON THE NEEDLE

4. REPEAT STEPS 1-3 UNTIL YOU HAVE CAST ON 16 (8) STITCHES

Now, let's get this adorable critter standing!

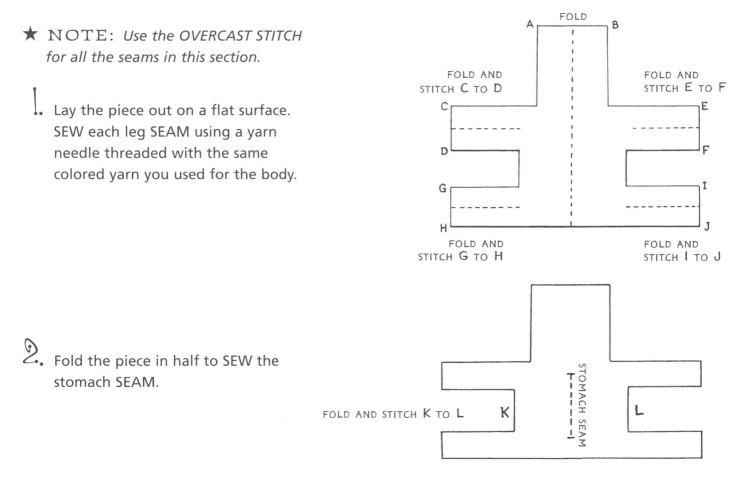

★ NOTE: *Use the OVERCAST STITCH for all the seams in this section.*

1. Lay the piece out on a flat surface. SEW each leg SEAM using a yarn needle threaded with the same colored yarn you used for the body.

2. Fold the piece in half to SEW the stomach SEAM.

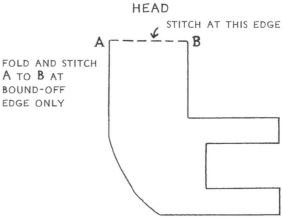

3. Turn the lamb inside out and stuff the legs with fleece (or wool) stuffing. (The eraser end of a pencil works great for this.)

4. Fold the head in half and SEW THE SEAMS together.

5. Beginning at the head seam, sew down toward the neck area with the threaded yarn needle and pull the yarn slowly. As you do this on both sides of the head, you'll see the lamb's head begin to take shape.

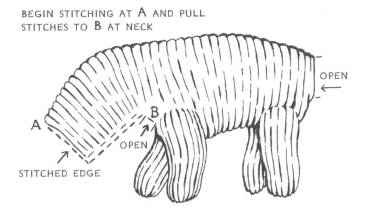

BEGIN STITCHING AT **A** AND PULL STITCHES TO **B** AT NECK

OPEN

OPEN

STITCHED EDGE

6. To finish making the lamb's face, tuck the extra folds of yarn inside the neck area and sew up the neck. Leave the chest area open to finish stuffing.

PUSH FOLDS OF KNITTING INTO NECK AND STITCH TO SECURE AFTER HEAD TAKES SHAPE

A

B

7. Finish stuffing the lamb, shaping it as you stuff. Make sure you add enough stuffing to the legs so the lamb can stand on its own.

8. SEW THE two remaining SEAMS.

MAKING THE TAIL

Using the off-white and black yarn, BRAID a tail about 4" (10 cm) long. Knot each end. Push one of the knots through the lamb and stitch it into place.

stretch your creative muscles!

*Make several little lambs to **give as presents**, to **decorate a tree**, or to **put on top of gift-wrapped packages**. You can also fill your little lambs with lavender or rose petals to **make sachets**.*

MAKING YOUR LAMB'S FACE

1. Cut two pieces of black felt 1" x ½" (2.5 x 1 cm). To form eyelashes, use a pair of scissors to cut slits along one of the long edges on each piece, stopping just short of the top edge.

   Glue the uncut top edge of each set of eyelashes to either side of your lamb's face.

FELT PIECE   ← SLIT UP TO THIS LINE

2. Cut two pieces of the off-white felt for ears. Glue one ear onto each side of your lamb's face.

3. Thread a yarn needle with a strand of the black yarn and stitch on the mouth.

❋ FINISHING TOUCHES ❋

Adding the ribbon

Tie a ribbon around your lamb's neck and finish it off with a bow. If you always want to know where your lamb is, attach a small bell to the ribbon under the lamb's neck.

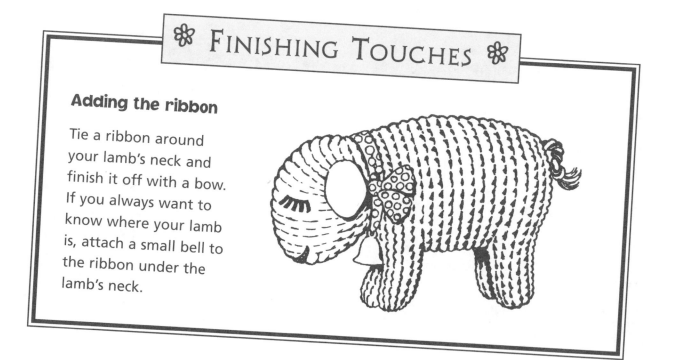

Perfect Purse

OK, I'll admit it! I'm a purse fanatic. I just plain love 'em, and I've got so many at home that I could open a store! The thing about purses is, they are so easy to knit and so versatile that I keep making them to give as gifts, too! I usually DOUBLE UP the YARN to make them sturdy enough to carry just about everything and anything.

Materials:

1 pair straight knitting needles, size 11

5-oz (125 g) skein of sport yarn, 2

Measuring tape or ruler

Sewing needle and matching thread

Button-style sew-on Velcro

Button, 2 (optional)

It's as simple as . . .

CAST ON (page 9)

KNIT STITCH (page 12)

PURL STITCH (page 14)

BIND OFF (page 16)

OVERCAST STITCH (page 62)

Here's the *basic pattern* for the Perfect Purse:

Row 1:
* Knit 1, Purl 1*; repeat * to end of row, ending with Purl 1

Row 2:
* Purl 1, Knit 1*; repeat * to end of row, ending with Knit 1

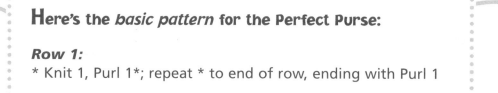

QUICK STARTS
how-to-knit-it

1. CAST ON 40 stitches using DOUBLED-UP YARN.

2. Work in the pattern until your piece measures 15" (37.5 cm) long.

3. BIND OFF all stitches. You now have a large rectangle. (To add a flap to your purse, make your rectangle longer. See page 47.)

4. Fold the rectangle in half. Both sides of your rectangle should look the same, so don't worry about which is the right or wrong side.

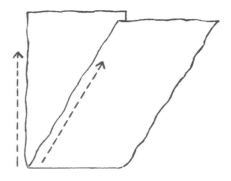

5. Using the OVERCAST STITCH, SEW THE SEAMS on both sides; WEAVE IN all loose ends. Then, turn the bag inside out.

DROPPED STITCHES SEVERAL ROWS BACK

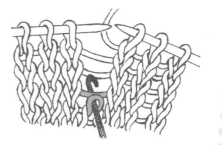

You already know how to fix dropped stitches in a current row or the row right below the current one (page 25). But what if you dropped a stitch several rows back and didn't notice it? If this happens, you'll notice a gap with lines of unknit yarn. You can fix this using a crochet hook!

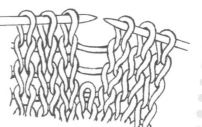

Slip the hook through the dropped stitch and grab the first line of yarn above the dropped stitch. Once you have the yarn snagged, pull it forward through the dropped stitch to create a loop. Now grab the next line of yarn with the crochet hook. As before, pull the line of unknit yarn forward, through the new loop, to create yet another loop.

Grab each line of yarn following these steps until you've made a loop with the top line of yarn. Now, slide this loop onto the left-hand needle. Great save! You're ready to continue knitting!

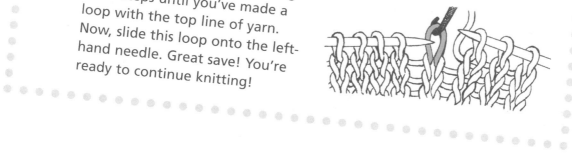

BRAIDING THE STRAP

Cut nine strands of yarn 36" (90 cm) long. Put them together and knot them at one end with some extra on the short side of the knot. Put the knotted end between your knees, separate the nine strands into three sets of three, and start BRAIDING. When you've finished braiding the yarn, make a knot at the other end, but leave some of the end yarn loose. Sew each knotted part to one of the top outside edges of your bag using a regular needle and thread that's the same color as your purse. The yarn that you left loose now hangs like fringe. How cool is that?

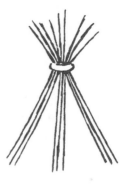

❋ FINISHING TOUCHES ❋

Adding the Velcro closure

To work properly, Velcro uses two pieces — a scratchy side and a fuzzy side. Place one piece of the Velcro (it doesn't matter which one you start with) *inside* the bag in the center near the top. Use your sewing needle and thread to attach the Velcro all around its edge. (Try not to push the sewing needle through to the other side of the purse.)

Sew the other half of the Velcro opposite the one you just attached.

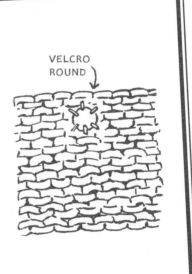

VELCRO
ROUND

⊚ **Add a beaded fringe** to the bottom edge of your purse (pages 27–28).

⊚ **Sew on sequins** in the shape of your initials.

⊚ **Add pretty ribbon roses** to the top edge of your purse or the bottom edge of the flap.

⊚ Why not **add a flap** to close up your purse? It's so easy, you've probably already thought of it yourself!

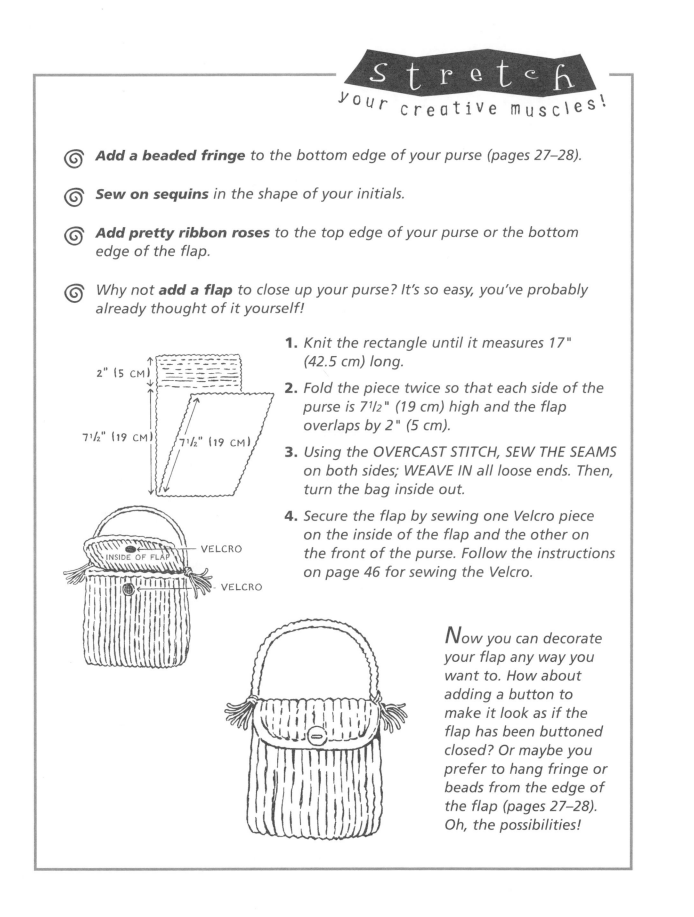

2" (5 CM)

7¹/₂" (19 CM)

7¹/₂" (19 CM)

VELCRO

INSIDE OF FLAP

VELCRO

1. Knit the rectangle until it measures 17" (42.5 cm) long.

2. Fold the piece twice so that each side of the purse is 7¹/₂" (19 cm) high and the flap overlaps by 2" (5 cm).

3. Using the OVERCAST STITCH, SEW THE SEAMS on both sides; WEAVE IN all loose ends. Then, turn the bag inside out.

4. Secure the flap by sewing one Velcro piece on the inside of the flap and the other on the front of the purse. Follow the instructions on page 46 for sewing the Velcro.

*N*ow you can decorate your flap any way you want to. How about adding a button to make it look as if the flap has been buttoned closed? Or maybe you prefer to hang fringe or beads from the edge of the flap (pages 27–28). Oh, the possibilities!

Sox & Stripes

You wear them to bed,
    You wear them to school,
You wear them out,
    Because they're so cool.

They're worn in the heel,
    They've thinned at the toe;
Now when you wear them,
    Your mother says, "No!"

So grab your best needles,
    Get yarn from the box,
Find the colors that suit you,
    And knit your own socks!

Materials:

1 pair straight knitting needles, size 6

Skeins of yarn in different colors, 3

Yarn needle

It's as simple as · · ·

CAST ON (page 9)

KNIT STITCH (page 12)

PURL STITCH (page 14)

DECREASE (page 60)

OVERCAST STITCH (page 62)

Here's the *basic pattern* **for Sox & Stripes:**

Knit 2, Purl 2; repeat * to end of row

QUICK STARTS
how-to-knit-it

1. CAST ON 48 stitches and work in the pattern, following the row sequence below (eight rows per color*).

Rows 1 to 8:	color #1	*Rows 33 to 40:*	color #2
Rows 9 to 16:	color #2	*Rows 41 to 48:*	color #3
Rows 17 to 24:	color #3	*Rows 49 to 56:*	color #1
Rows 25 to 32:	color #1	*Rows 57 to 64:*	color #2

* See page 52 for instructions on changing yarn colors.

2. Beginning with row 65, work the pattern with color #3 until the sock measures 16" (40 cm) long.

3. Now, to make the toe of the sock, DECREASE the number of stitches:

Row 65:   *KNIT 2 TOGETHER, PURL 2 TOGETHER*; repeat * to end of row until 24 stitches remain on the needle

Row 66:   *Knit 1, Purl 1*; repeat * to end of row

Rows 67 to 71:   Repeat row 2

Row 72:   KNIT 2 TOGETHER to end of row until 12 stitches remain

Row 73:   Knit 12 stitches

4. From your WORKING YARN, cut a long yarn tail. Thread it through the yarn needle and work it back through the 12 stitches remaining on the knitting needle. Remove the knitting needle and pull the yarn tail to close up the toe.

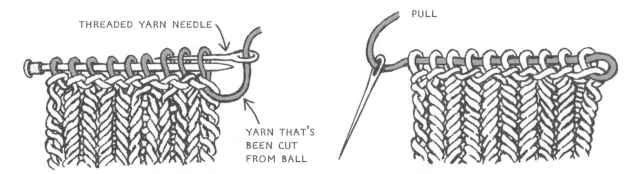

THREADED YARN NEEDLE

YARN THAT'S BEEN CUT FROM BALL

PULL

5. Now you can use the OVERCAST STITCH to SEW THE SEAM of your sock. Just make sure to rethread the yarn needle with a matching yarn tail when the colors change. When you've finished the seam, WEAVE IN all loose yarn ends and turn the sock right side out. You'll stop traffic with your bold stripes!

HOW MANY ROWS HAVE I WORKED?

Losing track of rows happens — no doubt about it! Here's how I keep track of rows worked: Keep paper and a pencil next to you. Write the row numbers on the left side of the paper, one under the other, from 1 to 8. To keep track of eight repeats, put a check next to each row *every time* you complete it until you have eight check marks for each one. The second time you use a color, put a slash through the check. The third time you use a color, circle the check. This will help you know where you are in the pattern at all times. Just be sure to always check off the row *after* you've knitted it! (Remember not to count the cast-on row.)

Can you guess where this knitter is in the pattern?

ANSWER: He just finished row 53.

ATTACHING A NEW COLOR YARN

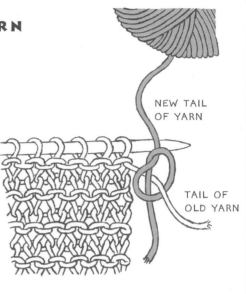

Though our instructions call for three colors, you can use as many or as few as you like. Just remember that it's easiest to change yarns when you reach the end of a row. Cut the WORKING YARN from the ball, leaving a tail 5" (12.5 cm) long. Tie the new yarn loosely onto the tail of the old yarn. Slide it up the tail as close as you can to the point where you'll make the first stitch of a new row. Continue knitting with the new yarn.

NEW TAIL OF YARN

TAIL OF OLD YARN

Stretch your creative muscles!

⊚ *With so many beautiful yarns available today, you may find it hard to narrow your choices!* **Check out the variegated (mixed colors) yarns** *available in almost any color you can imagine! If you find some variegated yarns that you like, try mixing and matching them with solid-colored yarns until you find a combination you like.*

⊚ **Make holiday socks** *for the whole family. It's fun on Christmas morning, for example, to have a new pair of socks in everyone's stocking. Be sure to take a picture!*

⊚ **Make socks in your school colors** *for your sports team or club.*

Tassel-Top Hat

Hats look terrific; hats are warm; hats hide bad-hair days! With your newfound knitting skills, why not make your own? Don't let today's fashions dictate what you make. Create your own fashion statement by knitting a hat in your favorite colors, and decorate it any way you want. Whatever you choose, "Hats off to you!"

Materials:

1 pair circular knitting needles, size 6

Small ball (about the size of a tennis ball) of contrasting-color yarn

3-oz (75 g) skein of main-color yarn

Yarn needle

Crochet hook

It's as simple as . . .

CAST ON (page 9)

PURL STITCH (page 14)

KNIT STITCH (page 12)

PURL 2 TOGETHER (page 60)

TWO-STITCH DECREASE (page 60)

KNIT 2 TOGETHER (page 60)

OVERCAST STITCH (page 62)

QUICK STARTS
how-to-knit-it

1. CAST ON 106 stitches with the contrasting-color yarn and work in the pattern, following the row sequence below.

Row 1: Purl all stitches.

Row 2: Knit all stitches.

Row 3: Knit all stitches and cut the yarn.

2. Before beginning the next row, attach the main-color yarn. (See "Attaching a New Color Yarn," page 52.)

Row 4: Purl all stitches.

Row 5: Purl all stitches.

Row 6: Knit all stitches.

Row 7: Purl all stitches.

Row 8: Knit all stitches.

Row 9: Purl all stitches.

Row 10: Knit all stitches.

Row 11: Purl all stitches.

Row 12: Knit all stitches.

Row 13: Purl all stitches; then, PURL 2 TOGETHER to DECREASE the row by one stitch. You should have 105 stitches remaining on your needle.

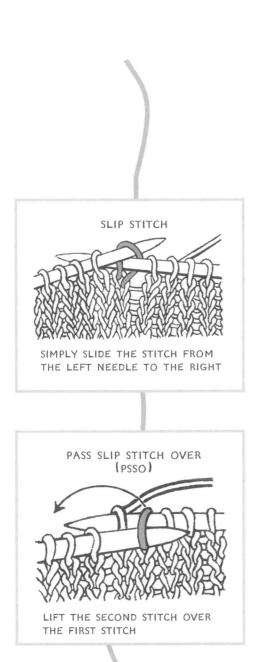

SLIP STITCH

SIMPLY SLIDE THE STITCH FROM
THE LEFT NEEDLE TO THE RIGHT

PASS SLIP STITCH OVER
(PSSO)

LIFT THE SECOND STITCH OVER
THE FIRST STITCH

SHAPING THE HAT

Row 14: Knit 9, *TWO-STITCH DECREASE (slip 1 stitch from the left needle to the right needle, KNIT 2 TOGETHER, and PASS SLIP STITCH OVER), Knit 18*, repeat * until there are 12 stitches left. To finish the row, TWO-STITCH DECREASE, Knit 9. There should be 95 stitches remaining on your needle.

Row 15: Purl all stitches.

Row 16: Knit all stitches.

Row 17: Purl all stitches.

Row 18: Knit 8, *TWO-STITCH DECREASE, Knit 16*, repeat * until there are 8 stitches left, Knit the last 8 stitches. There should be 85 stitches remaining on the needle.

Row 19: Purl all stitches.

Row 20: Knit all stitches.

Row 21: Purl all stitches.

Row 22: Knit 7, *TWO-STITCH DECREASE, Knit 14*, repeat * until there are 7 stitches left, Knit the last 7 stitches. There should be 75 stitches remaining on the needle.

Row 23: Purl all stitches.

Row 24: Knit all stitches.

Row 25: Purl all stitches.

Row 26: Knit 6, *TWO-STITCH DECREASE, Knit 12*, repeat * until there are 6 stitches left, Knit the last 6 stitches. There should be 65 stitches remaining on the needle.

Row 27: Purl all stitches.

Row 28: Knit all stitches.

Row 29: Purl all stitches.

SHAPING THE CROWN

Row 30:   Knit all stitches, then cut yarn.

Row 31:   Attach contrasting color. Knit all stitches, then cut yarn.

Row 32:   Attach main color. Purl all stitches.

Row 33:   Purl all stitches, PURL the last 2 stitches TOGETHER to DECREASE the row by one stitch. There should be 64 stitches remaining on the needle.

Row 34:   *Knit 6 stitches, KNIT 2 TOGETHER*, repeat * to end of row.

Row 35:   Purl 56 stitches.

Row 36:   *Knit 5 stitches, KNIT 2 TOGETHER *, repeat * to end of row.

Row 37:   Purl 48 stitches.

Row 38:   *Knit 4 stitches, KNIT 2 TOGETHER *, repeat * to end of row.

Row 39:   Purl 40 stitches.

Row 40:   *Knit 3 stitches, KNIT 2 TOGETHER *, repeat * to end of row.

Row 41:   Purl 32 stitches.

Row 42:   *Knit 2 stitches, KNIT 2 TOGETHER *, repeat * to end of row.

Row 43:   Purl 24 stitches.

Row 44:   *KNIT 2 TOGETHER *, repeat to end of row. There should be 12 stitches remaining on the needle. Cut a tail 12" (30 cm) long for sewing the hat seam.

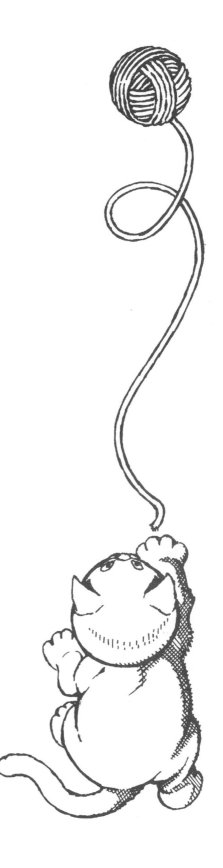

SEWING THE SEAM

Thread the yarn tail through a yarn needle and run it back through the 12 stitches left on the knitting needle.

THREADED YARN NEEDLE

YARN THAT'S BEEN CUT FROM BALL

PULL

Pull the yarn tail to close the opening at the top of your hat; then, use the OVERCAST STITCH to sew the seam from the top of the hat down to the beginning edge. When you reach the point where the color changes, use the contrasting-color yarn to sew that part of the seam.

To add a tassel, see page 58.

Stretch *your creative muscles!*

⊚ **BRAID thick yarn** about 8" (20 cm) long. Attach at the crown and let it hang down. Create several strands of long, beaded fringe (pages 27–28) and let them hang from the crown.

⊚ **Sew on appliqués or emblems** to the front of your hat.

⊚ When you pull the yarn to close the crown of your hat, **leave an opening to pull your ponytail through**.

❄ FINISHING TOUCHES ❄

Making the tassel

1. Cut a piece of cardboard 4" x 4" (10 x 10 cm). Loosely wind the yarn around the cardboard several times. With a separate piece of yarn, tie all of the wound yarn at the top, as shown, and cut across the bottom.

2. Wind another piece of cut yarn around your tassel about 1/2" (1 cm) from the knot at the top. Tie the ends in a knot and smooth them into the other strands of the tassel.

3. Place the tassel on top of the hat. Push the crochet hook from inside the hat out to the top, grab the yarn ends, and pull them through. Secure the tassel by knotting the ends. WEAVE them IN through the inside stitches.

Here's your hat ...

    and what a hat it is!

TASSEL

OUTSIDE OF HAT

KNOT YARN ENDS AND WEAVE IN

INSIDE OF HAT

Quick Starts
Illustrated Stitch &
How-To Dictionary

ADDING STITCHES
See INCREASING.

BIND OFF
For an illustrated guide to binding off, see pages 16–18.

BRAIDING
Start with three strands. Take the far left piece and bring it
to the middle of the other two pieces by crossing it in front.
Then, take the far right piece and bring it to the middle, also
crossing it in front. Repeat left to middle, right to middle
until you have a braid that's as long as you want it to be.

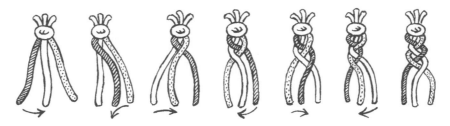

CAST ON
For an illustrated guide to casting on, see pages 9–10.

CONTINOUS STITCH

See SEW THE SEAMS.

DECREASING

To reduce the number of stitches in a row, you can knit or purl two stitches together so they become one stitch!

Knit 2 Together

Insert the right needle into two stitch loops and knit them together. You've just decreased your row by one stitch!

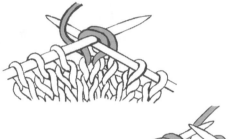

Purl 2 Together

Insert the right needle into two stitch loops and purl them together. Voilà — one purl decrease made!

Two-Stitch Decrease

This method enables you to decrease while creating a crisscross pattern.

Step 1: SLIP one STITCH (see SLIP STITCH).

Step 2: KNIT 2 TOGETHER (see DECREASING).

Step 3: PASS SLIP STITCH OVER (See PASS SLIP STITCH OVER)

DOUBLED-UP YARN

For an explanation of doubled-up yarn, see page 32.

INCREASING

"Increasing" enables you to create two knit or purl stitches where you only had one.

Knit Increase

Step 1: Insert the right needle into the stitch to be increased. Proceed as if you were going to knit, keeping the stitch on the left needle.

Step 2: Pull the right needle a little bit toward you to create a small loop. (This will give you some room to move your right needle.) It will look like you have a stitch on both the right needle and left needle. Now, switch the position of your needles so your right needle is in back of the left needle. Insert the right needle into the back of the same stitch on the left and complete the knit stitch. That's all there is to it — one knit increase made!

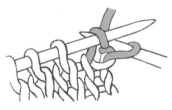

Purl Increase

Step 1: Purl a stitch, keeping the stitch on the left needle. Give a tiny tug on the right needle to create some room to move.

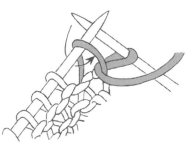

Step 2: Insert the needle into the back loop of the same stitch and complete the purl stitch. One purl increase made!

INVISIBLE STITCH

See SEW THE SEAMS.

KNIT STITCH

For an illustrated guide to the knit stitch, see page 12.

KNIT 2 TOGETHER

See DECREASING.

PASS SLIP STITCH OVER (PSSO)

This is very similar to the bind off explained earlier, but is used as a way to decrease with a little slant to the left, creating a pattern within a pattern.

Step 1: Slip Stitch

Knit Slip Stitch

Insert the right needle into a stitch as if you were going to knit it. However, instead of knitting it, simply slip it from the left needle to the right needle.

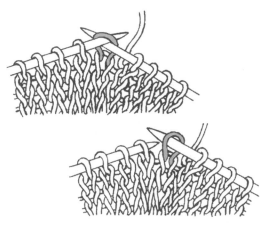

Purl Slip Stitch

Insert the right needle into the stitch as if to purl, but instead of purling it, simply slip it from the left needle to the right needle.

Step 2: Pass Over

Knit or purl the next stitch (depending on how the pattern reads) until it's completed and on the right needle. Then, use the left needle to carry the slipped stitch over the one just worked and around the tip of the right needle. (You'll probably notice that the tip of the right needle is hooking the second stitch through the first one.) If you've learned how to bind off, then this probably feels very familiar!

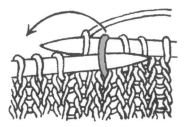

OVERCAST STITCH

See SEW THE SEAMS.

PURL STITCH

For an illustrated guide to the purl stitch, see page 14.

READING PATTERNS

For an explanation of reading patterns, see page 18.

SEW THE SEAMS

There are several ways to join seams. Here are illustrations showing the invisible stitch, the overcast stitch, and the continuous stitch.

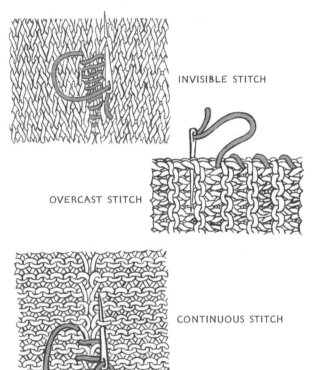

INVISIBLE STITCH

OVERCAST STITCH

CONTINUOUS STITCH

SLIP STITCH

A stitch that results when you simply slide one stitch from the left needle to the right needle without knitting or purling it.

TWO-STITCH DECREASE

See DECREASING.

WEAVE IN

After sewing all of the seams, weave in all the loose yarn threads. If there are threads along a seam, use an embroidery or yarn needle to thread them through the seam or along the edges of the piece on the wrong side.

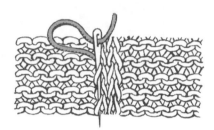

If you have yarn ends that are not near any seams, weave them through the backs of stitches (always on the wrong side) in an uneven pattern.

WORKING YARN

The yarn from the ball or skein, which is the yarn you are working into the knitted project.

INDEX